methadone maintenance treatment

client handbook

REVISED

Centre for Addiction and Mental Health
Centre de toxicomanie et de santé mentale

*A Pan American Health Organization /
World Health Organization
Collaborating Centre*

**Methadone Maintenance Treatment
Client Handbook**
REVISED

ISBN: 978-0-88868-699-2 (PRINT)
ISBN: 978-0-88868-700-5 (PDF)
ISBN: 978-0-88868-701-2 (HTML)
ISBN: 978-0-88868-922-1 (ePUB)

Printed in Canada

This publication may be available in other formats. For information
about alternative formats or other CAMH publications, or to place an
order, please contact Sales and Distribution:
Toll-free: 1 800 661-1111
Toronto: 416 595-6059
E-mail: publications@camh.ca
Online store: http://store.camh.net

Website: www.camh.ca

Disponible en français sous le titre :
Traitement de maintien à la méthadone : Manuel du client

4855a / 03-2013 / PZ160

acknowledgments

The Centre for Addiction and Mental Health (CAMH) wishes to acknowledge the valuable and enthusiastic participation of methadone clients from across Ontario in the development of this handbook. Clients suggested what information we should include, they provided us with straight-up quotations about their experience and advice, and they reviewed and commented on the draft copy. Their involvement helped us to create a book that we believe will interest, inform and empower methadone clients throughout *Ontario. Due to the restrictions of confidentiality we cannot list* the names of the many clients who participated in the project, so instead we offer this expression of our earnest appreciation and gratitude for their contribution.

CAMH Project Team
Michelle Maynes, Writer
Garth Martin, Project Manager, Methadone Treatment
    Dissemination Project
Andrew Johnson, Product Developer

Advisory Committee
Anne Bowlby, Ontario Substance Abuse Bureau
Larry Corea/Diane Smylie, Breakaway — Parkdale Satellite
Jim Hanna, Newport Centre
Jeff Ostofsky, Methadone Works
Kate Tschakovsky, CAMH

Additional Project Consultants
Wayne Charles, Counsellor, CAMH Opiate Clinic, Toronto
Frederick W. Christie, Advocates for the Integration of Recovery &
    Methadone (AFIRM)

Continued...

Additional Project Consultants *(continued)*
Dr. Paul Humphries, Senior Medical Consultant, Ministry of Solicitor
   General and Ministry of Correctional Services
Sarah Hutchison, Methadone Registry, College of Physicians
   and Surgeons
Pearl Isaac, Pharmacist, CAMH, Toronto
Anne Kalvik, Pharmacist, CAMH, Toronto
Scott Macdonald, Scientist, CAMH, Toronto
Nancy Sutton, Correctional Service Canada
Joycelyn Woods, National Alliance of Methadone Advocates

Professional Reviewers
Dr. Bruna Brands, Clinical Trials Scientist, Toronto
Dr. Tony Hammer, Physician, Windsor
Dr. Luc Laroche, Physician, Ottawa
Dr. David Marsh, Clinical Director, Addiction Medicine Program,
   Toronto
Staff of Stonehenge Therapeutic Community, Guelph

Client Interviews
Miranda Borisenko, CAMH, Hamilton
Mark Erdelyan, CAMH, Windsor
Andrew Johnson, CAMH, Toronto
Lyle Nicol, CAMH, Thunder Bay
Peter Williams, CAMH, Ottawa

CAMH Creative Services
Bob Tarjan, Book Design
Sue McCluskey, Copy Editor
Nancy Leung, Creative Services Co-ordinator
Christine Harris, Production Co-ordinator

2008 Edition Acknowledgements
The 2008 edition of the Client Handbook would not have been
possible without the support and expertise of Dr. Anita Srivastava,
CAMH Addiction Medicine Clinic; Pearl Isaac, CAMH Pharmacy;
Dr. Bruna Brands, Health Canada; Chantal Degranges, College
of Physicians and Surgeons of Ontario; Michelle Maynes, CAMH
Publication Developer; Krystyna Ross, CAMH, Manager, Publication
Services and Creative Services; and Betty Dondertman, CAMH,
Manager, Education Services and Web Strategies.

The 2008 edition project was managed by Andrew Johnson, CAMH
Publication Developer. Editorial, graphics and translation work was
carried out, respectively, by Jacquelyn Waller-Vintar, Bob Tarjan
and Evelyne Barthès-McDonald.

contents

how to use this book

When the methadone clients at the Opiate Clinic at the Centre for Addiction and Mental Health (CAMH) were asked what they wanted from a client handbook, they said they wanted a book that would give them all the information they needed in one place. They wanted something that would set the record straight on the length of treatment, side-effects, other drugs, counselling, pregnancy, travel, withdrawal and ending treatment. They wanted quotations from clients. They wanted it to be easy to read.

This book should answer many of the questions you may have about methadone treatment, and can help you to know what questions you should ask your doctor, pharmacist, counsellor and others. It's put together so that you can either dip into it, or read it all at once, as you wish. There's information here for those thinking about methadone treatment, for the new client and the long-term client, and for families and friends. You can use this information to help you to understand and make decisions about your treatment. You can use it to educate others. You can use it to help yourself get well.

methadone myths and realities

MYTH: *Methadone will get you high.*

REALITY: If you're looking for a high, you'll be *disappointed with methadone. When you first start* treatment, you may feel lightheaded or sleepy for a few days, but you will quickly develop a tolerance to these effects. Expect to feel "normal" when you're on methadone.

MYTH: *Methadone will make you sick.*

REALITY: The only time you might feel sick from methadone is at the beginning of your treatment, when your dose might not be enough to keep you free of withdrawal symptoms. In most cases, if you do feel sick, it's mild. Your dose will be adjusted and you should feel better within a few days.

When you're on methadone you can catch a cold or any other illness just like anyone else, but you're much less prone to illness than illicit drug users. People on methadone are less likely to use needles, and more likely to eat well and take good care of themselves.

When you're on methadone you won't wake up sick every morning. If anything, methadone will help you to get well.

MYTH: *Long-term use of methadone damages the liver, the thyroid gland and the memory.*

REALITY: Long-term use of methadone is safe. It will not damage your internal organs, and when you are on the correct dose, it will not interfere with your thinking. If you have a medical condition such as hepatitis or cirrhosis of the liver, methadone maintenance treatment can improve your access to medical treatment, and help you to manage the illness.

MYTH: *Methadone rots your teeth and bones.*

REALITY: This is a common myth, and although it's not true, the reasons behind the myth deserve some consideration.

One of the side-effects of methadone, like many medications, is that it gives you a dry mouth. This can make your teeth more prone to the production of plaque, which is a major cause of gum disease and tooth decay. To protect your teeth, follow the dental *routine recommended for everyone: brush and floss* every day, rinse your mouth with mouthwash, go to the dentist at least twice a year, and cut sugar from your diet. Drinking plenty of water can also help to relieve dry mouth.

If you're on methadone, and you feel like your bones are rotting, it's probably because you're on too low a dose. Bone ache, which may feel like bone "rot," is a symptom of methadone withdrawal. When your dose is adjusted correctly you should not experience any aching or other symptoms of withdrawal.

MYTH: *Methadone makes you gain weight.*
REALITY: Not everyone gains weight when they go on methadone, but some do. This is usually because methadone improves your health and appetite, and so you eat more. If you've been using drugs for a long time, you may be underweight and need to gain a few pounds.

Even though the methadone drink is not "fattening" like sweets and fatty foods, methadone can slow your metabolism and cause water retention, which can lead to weight gain. You can control weight gain by choosing healthy foods that are high *in fibre such as whole grains and fruits and vegetables,* and by exercising regularly. If you nourish your body, you'll keep the pounds off, and more important, you'll feel good.

MYTH: *It's easy to get off methadone / It's hard to get off methadone.*
REALITY: How could these both be myths? Well it isn't easy to get off methadone, but it doesn't have to be hard either. The symptoms of methadone withdrawal come on more slowly than those of heroin withdrawal, but with methadone, the withdrawal process takes longer. When you are ready to go off methadone, your

dose will be "tapered," or gradually reduced, usually
at a rate that you determine. (For more information on
ending methadone treatment, see page 113.)

MYTH: *People on methadone are still addicts, even if
they don't use any other drugs.*

REALITY: People who take methadone as a treatment
for opioid dependence are no more addicts than are
people who take insulin as a treatment for diabetes.
Methadone is a medication. Methadone treatment
allows you to live a normal life, work, go to school,
or care for your children.

MYTH: *Methadone is a cure for opioid addiction.*

REALITY: Methadone is not a cure; it is a tool that helps
you to repair the damage caused by dependence, and
to build a new life. Like any tool, you have to use it.
Just as a builder uses a hammer to frame a house, or
an artist uses a brush to paint a picture, you can use
methadone to help you steer clear of drugs. Methadone
will make the job easier, but it won't make it easy.

"I should have started the methadone program ten years ago but I didn't because of all the ignorance and all the talk, like you're still addicted and methadone gets you high, and blah blah blah blah. So I wasted ten years of my life trying therapies where there was total abstinence. For me it only worked for a year and half and then I fell back into drugs and I was even more miserable and more bitter because the program didn't work. What helped me was methadone..."

— Marco
On methadone 15 months

"The whole stereotype that surrounds methadone prevents so many people from getting involved. People need methadone, and they're afraid of it. The medical community should be knowledgeable about the program; they should support it. My family doctor apologized to me; she said, 'I'm sorry I recommended you for the methadone program because I only changed you from one kind of junkie to another.' A doctor! It's really sad; I mean, what other choice do we have? Cold turkey? You might be successful for a while... People need to know that methadone is okay, that it works."

— Beth, 39
On methadone four years

1 methadone and other options

1 methadone and other options

Is methadone maintenance treatment for you?

If you've been using opioid drugs such as heroin, OxyContin, codeine, Dilaudid, Percocet and others, and you've come to a point where you know you can't go on using, but you can't seem to stop either, methadone maintenance treatment (MMT) may be right for you.

If you're pregnant, and you're using heroin, seek MMT right away. Methadone prevents opioid withdrawal, which can threaten the life of your baby (turn to page 106).

Users who are HIV or hepatitis C positive are strongly urged to begin methadone treatment immediately. MMT helps to stabilize your health, and it lets you focus on getting the best possible care (see page 71).

You may be ready for MMT if you've been using for a year or more, and you've tried to stop. You've been through withdrawal, you've seen a counsellor, perhaps you've gone through a residential treatment program. If you can't seem to stop using for more than a few hours, days, weeks or months at a time, and you know you want to stop, think about going on MMT.

You're ready for MMT when you're still using and all it's doing for you is keeping you "normal." If there's any high at all, it isn't worth it anymore. You're scared of being sick and all you want is to feel well and be free of the craving that nags you to keep on using. You want to be more in control of your life, your work, your home. You want to feel better about yourself; you want to be able to offer more to the people you care about.

If you think you're ready for MMT, read through this *handbook to find out what it is, how it works, what to* expect and where to go. Pass this handbook on to your family and friends to help them understand and be able to offer you the support you need.

Treatment programs vary, so be prepared to ask questions. The more you know, the more you'll be in control of getting where you want to go. *Help is available.*

> **❝** *I wish I had kept a diary from just before I started methadone, then every time I am having a difficult time, I could re-read my thoughts and know that I do not want to return to that place.* **❞**
>
> — Adam, 20
> On methadone three months

The benefits of MMT

For people who are dependant on opioids, *methadone has a number of benefits over other* opioids. These are:

- The effects of methadone can last 24 to 36 hours. For most people, as long as you take your one dose a day at the same time every day, you won't get sick with opioid withdrawal.

- You drink your dose of methadone, usually in a mixture with orange juice. Taking an oral dose is much safer than injecting, snorting or smoking.

- Drinking methadone won't get you high, but it can help to keep away the physical drug cravings, or the feeling that you need to get high. Some people experience no cravings at all once they're on methadone. Others may continue to struggle with the "conditioned" cravings, or those that are triggered by something or someone you associate with drug use. The counselling you can get with MMT can help make it easier to cope with cravings.

- When prescribed by a doctor and dispensed by a pharmacist, methadone is legal. The source is reliable and safe, and there's no fear of arrest.

- Methadone is made using strict manufacturing guidelines. The exact potency is known, and it's never cut with unknown substances. You know what you're getting.

- The cost of methadone is less than $10 a day. If you *have an Ontario Drug Benefit Card, or are covered* by a prescription drug plan at your work, or through a member of your family, methadone costs you nothing. *You may also qualify for financial* assistance through the Trillium Drug Plan. (For more information on help with the cost, see page 49.)

- Some illicit-drug users participate in a lifestyle that involves crime and other risky activities to support their need for drugs. Methadone replaces this need with a substance that is legal and cheap. Methadone treatment can result in less crime, fewer people in jail and a safer community.

- People on methadone are less likely to use or share needles. If you're not using needles, the risk of becoming infected with HIV or hepatitis C is reduced. And since methadone lets you think straight and use your head, you'll be more likely to practice all you know about safe sex.

- Methadone blocks the euphoric effect of other opioid drugs. For example, if you take a hit of heroin when you're on methadone, you may not feel it. *Methadone's opioid-blocking effect can be a benefit* because it takes away the main reasons why you might continue to use other opioids. If you can't get high, and you won't get sick if you don't use, why waste your money?

- Going on methadone treatment can put you in touch with people who understand where you're at, and can help you get where you want to go.

- Once you've been on methadone for a while, you should feel more energetic and clear-headed. This lets you focus your life on things like work, school and family.

- Of all treatments for opioid dependence, MMT has the best record for keeping clients off other opioid drugs.

"Methadone worked for me, but I knew what I wanted when I went on it: to live without heroin for life. It did help me to do that. I've been abstinent from all other drugs for nine years.

If you want methadone to work for you, you've got to make the decision and follow it through. You need will, desire and determination. You need to have a positive attitude, you need to have self-respect.

My reward has been the chance to enjoy my family, to find employment, to have good health in my mind and body, and to be in control, for once, of my own happiness. I've learned a lot about myself. I'm friendlier and more helpful to others. I love me now, and I love life! "

— Margaret, 41

On methadone 11 years

The drawbacks of MMT

- Methadone is not a cure for opioid dependence; it is a treatment. For it to work, you've got to *want* it to work. Success requires motivation and determination.

- Methadone treatment replaces opioids such as heroin, OxyContin and codeine with another opioid, methadone. You are still opioid dependent, and if you miss more than one dose, you will experience *flu-like withdrawal symptoms.*

- Methadone clients may be branded as "still addicted" by some members of the community. Many people don't understand methadone treatment, even some people who work in the addiction and health professions. Some drug treatment programs and self-help groups like Narcotics Anonymous (NA) are abstinence-based, and may not accept methadone clients. Some doctors and pharmacists are reluctant to work with methadone clients, perhaps fearing they will be pressured to supply prescription drugs. Some employers may not react kindly if they discover that you're a methadone client. It's probably fair to say that *most* people regard methadone treatment as a positive step, but there will be exceptions, and you should be prepared for that.

- While methadone *detox* is sometimes used to withdraw opioid users by reducing their opioid dose gradually over a short term, methadone *maintenance* is a long-term treatment. You can expect to be on it for at least a year or two. Some stay on for as long as 20 years or more. In general, the longer you've been dependent on opioids, the longer you'll likely stay on methadone. Other factors include how long you *want* to stay on methadone, and how things are with your family, home and work life.

- As it stands now, methadone treatment guidelines say *that for the first few months of treatment you have* to go to the clinic or pharmacy every day to get your dose. Even after a year of treatment, you still have to go at least once a week. Expect to make a lot of visits to your doctor too.

- You will be asked to produce samples of your urine for drug testing frequently. It's often required that these samples be produced "under observation," meaning someone will be watching you to be sure that the urine is yours, and that you haven't done anything to change it.

- Methadone can have some unpleasant side-effects. These are likely to be more pronounced at the beginning of treatment — during the two- to six-week dose stabilization phase when you may experience withdrawal symptoms. The most frequently reported side-effects include drowsiness and light-headedness, nausea and vomiting, excessive sweating, constipation and change in sex drive. Other complaints include insomnia and agitation, joint pain and swelling, ankle swelling, skin rash, dry mouth and weakness. Often an adjustment to your dose will help to reduce side-effects. Always report side-effects to your doctor and pharmacist.

- Even though methadone blocks the opioid high, some people do continue to use other opioids on occasion when they start methadone treatment. Seeking out the opioid high when you're on methadone can be dangerous. Methadone is a strong opioid drug, and if you take more opioids, you might not feel high, but you'll be at risk of overdose. Talk to your doctor about using other opioids. If you feel the need to take additional opioids it may mean that your methadone dose should be adjusted.

My advice to those who want to go on meth is think good and hard and consider other alternatives. Methadone is not a drug to get high on, and it has severe side-effects. It should not be taken lightly.

— Margaret, 41
On methadone 11 years

> *I wish I'd known when I went on meth that it would be a lifelong hell. It's a ball and chain.*
>
> — David, 36
> On methadone four years

> *Methadone is not a lifelong hell! And it's not a ball and chain — unless you make it that way. If you get your shit together and it's in your fridge, you can go about your life the same as anyone else. You wake up in the morning and you take it, just like you brush your teeth and you drink your coffee.*
>
> — Richard, 45
> On methadone three years

Other treatment options

As you can see, for all its benefits, methadone does have its drawbacks. Before you decide to commit to long-term methadone treatment, consider these other treatment options.

Withdrawal/detoxification

*You probably know about cold turkey, that horrible flu-*like sickness that makes it so hard to kick. What you may not know is that there are ways of reducing the withdrawal symptoms, making the process easier to get through (see below). While some things can help, the most important factor in getting through withdrawal is time. Over time the sickness goes away, and the cravings come less often.

Remember that detoxification, in itself, is rarely enough to bring an end to a history of habitual drug use. When combined with a drug rehabilitation *program, detoxification can be successful, especially* if you are highly motivated to get off drugs.

The following options for assistance in withdrawal and *detoxification can be discussed with your doctor:*

- Clonidine is a prescription drug that can reduce symptoms of opioid withdrawal. It lowers your blood pressure, which can also lower your energy level, so if you take it, be prepared to rest. Ask your doctor about other non-opioid drugs (such as anti-*inflammatories, antidiarrheals and antinauseants)* that can help control symptoms of withdrawal.

- Methadone detox involves establishing a stable dose of methadone, and then gradually decreasing the dose until withdrawal is complete. This process may be completed within one month, or can take up to six months. Some may decide once they are on methadone that they prefer to continue with the treatment, rather than taper off.

- Acupuncture can sometimes help to relieve withdrawal symptoms, especially for those whose opioid dependence is on the milder end of the scale.

The treatment involves the insertion of stainless steel disposable acupuncture needles into the ears.
It is believed that the needles can stimulate the release of endorphins, chemicals in the brain that help to relieve withdrawal symptoms.

- *Rapid opioid detoxification is a controversial and* expensive experimental procedure that has high rates of relapse. The process involves going under *general anaesthetic for five to six hours. While you* are asleep, you are given a number of drugs, including naltrexone. Naltrexone is an opioid antagonist, a drug that prevents opioids from having any effect. This causes you to go into intense withdrawal. Providers of the service may claim the treatment speeds up the withdrawal process, but
you can still expect to experience significant withdrawal symptoms when you wake up. The treatment includes continuing with the naltrexone. Anyone considering this treatment should question whether the risks of undergoing anaesthetic, and the *cost, are justified. It is not a miracle cure.*

- Following withdrawal, the drug naltrexone may be helpful in reducing the temptation to use again. Naltrexone blocks the opioid receptors in the brain, which means that even if you take opioids, you won't get high. Naltrexone is also used in the treatment of alcohol dependence. Naltrexone is available as a pill that can be taken daily. Naltrexone is non-addictive, and will not cause withdrawal when stopped.

Narcotics Anonymous

Based on the 12-step program of Alcoholics Anonymous, Narcotics Anonymous (NA) is an association of recovering drug addicts with groups in many countries around the world.

NA members gather at informal meetings to share their personal experiences of drug addiction. The principle behind the organization is that those who have experienced drug dependence, and have found *a way to deal with it, are the most qualified to offer* support and advice to others who wish to do the same. The 12-step approach hinges on the belief that those who are addicted are powerless over drugs, and that *through faith, reflection, reconciliation and helping* others, sanity is restored.

While NA's only stated requirement of member-ship is "a desire to stop using drugs," they do encourage complete abstinence from all drugs, including alcohol.

Some NA groups are supportive of methadone clients and will encourage you to participate. Others may welcome you at NA meetings, but won't invite you to participate. (Some people get around this by simply not mentioning that they're on methadone.) NA members are encouraged to be drug-free, but people on methadone maintenance are committed to a long-term, drug-based treatment. Similar groups, called Methadone Anonymous, are aimed at methadone clients, and are forming in some centres. (See page 96 for more information on Methadone Anonymous.)

ConnexOntario's drug and alcohol registry of treatment *will provide you with a local number to call to find the* NA meetings nearest to you. Call their 24-hour toll-free line at 1-800-565-8603.

Alternative addiction self-help

For those who are motivated to give up drugs, and who may not be comfortable with the 12-step approach, there are a growing number of alternative approaches to addiction recovery. Check the Web or your local library for information about approaches such as Rational Recovery and SMART (Self-Management and Recovery Training).

Day/evening and residential treatment

Day/evening or residential treatment programs for substance abuse are available across Ontario. Residential programs can be short term (less than 40 days) or long term (more than 40 days). Generally both day/evening and residential treatment are structured programs offering intensive individual and group therapy. Some long-term residential programs allow you to work or attend school while receiving treatment.

All residential treatment programs require that you be drug-free prior to admission, however more and more of them are accepting methadone clients.

To explore the options of day/evening or residential treatment, contact your local assessment and referral *service (find the number by calling ConnexOntario's* drug and alcohol registry of treatment at 1-800-565-8603) or talk to your doctor or counsellor.

Buprenorphine

Buprenorphine is one of the first new treatment options for opioid dependence since methadone was introduced in Canada over 40 years ago. Buprenorphine is similar to methadone in that it reduces drug cravings, blocks the effect of opioid drugs and suppresses withdrawal symptoms. Buprenorphine is regarded as an alternative to methadone and is not seen as a treatment that will replace methadone. For more information, talk to your doctor about the availability of buprenorphine (also called Suboxone) and ask if it is the right medication for you.

Weighing your options

Methadone maintenance has the best record in terms of keeping clients in treatment and off opioid drugs for the longest period of time. On the other hand, it does carry some side-effects that may be unpleasant, and it does require a long-term commitment. If you have tried one or more of the other treatment options listed, and you are still using, and you know you want to stop, methadone may be your best choice.

2 learning about methadone

2 learning about methadone

What's an opiate, what's an opioid?

The term "opiate" refers to drugs derived from the opium poppy, such as opium, morphine and codeine, and to drugs that are derived from the opium poppy and then chemically altered, such as heroin. The term "opioid" is like a family name that includes opiates, and also other drugs that have morphine-like effects, but are not made from the opium poppy. These drugs are made by chemists in labs, and include methadone, Demerol, OxyContin, Percocet, Dilaudid and others.

How do opioid drugs work?

Endorphins

Your body produces its own opioid drugs, called endorphins. Endorphins are your body's natural painkillers.

Inside your brain is a number of what are called "pain receptors." Their job is to tell you when pain is happening in your body. For example, if someone steps on your toe, your pain receptors light up and you cry "Ow."

At first the pain is quite intense, but by the time the toe stepper is telling you how sorry he or she is, it doesn't hurt quite so much. While your pain receptors have told you to feel pain, they are also signalling to your endorphins to come and relieve the pain. The *endorphins "fill up" your pain receptors, so in a few* minutes the pain in your toe seems trivial.

Endorphins can boost your mood too, and affect how you respond to situations of stress. Exercise is a great way to release endorphins. Take a closer look at those all-weather joggers you see running around the park every day. See the sweat pouring off them, see the glow in their faces. They're hooked on "runner's high."

Opioids

What happens if you fall and break your arm? Your body won't produce enough endorphins to knock out that much pain. Inside your brain many of your pain receptors are still empty, and they're screaming out *to be filled with something to take away the pain.*

In situations like this, it's fortunate that opioid drugs *can fill up the pain receptors in the same way as* endorphins. What's more, the strength of the opioid drug and the dose can be adjusted to address the intensity of pain, as needed. You might be moaning and groaning when you get to the hospital, but once your doctor gives you a shot of morphine, you can sit there and be reasonably comfortable while he or she sets your broken arm and puts it in a cast. Before you go home, he or she gives you a prescription for codeine pills, so you won't have to suffer while the arm gets better.

For most people, a situation like this would be the only time they take opioid drugs. Once the arm begins to heal and the pain becomes tolerable, they stop taking the codeine, and don't give it a second thought.

Opioid dependence

But what if the pain doesn't go away? What if the only thing that can bring relief is opioid drugs? You might continue to take them, and since you like the way they make you feel, you get some more. After a while, if they're not working as well as they used to, you take more at a time, or you try a stronger opioid. You think you can stop when you want to, but when you do try to stop, you get sick, and can't stop thinking about starting up again. Eventually much of your time, energy and interest may be absorbed in getting and taking drugs. Your body has adapted to having the drugs, and now you feel like you have to have them.

This is, of course, only one way that opioid dependence can begin. Some get into it for kicks, seeking out *new experience and finding one that is pleasurable and* predictable, for a while. Some are seeking relief from the daily grind of poverty, from emotional hardship or from depression. Some may be drawn to the reckless image of the drugs, wanting to see themselves as "cool" or "hip."

Once you get into it, you may go on using for a long time, knowing that it's dangerous, knowing that the *pleasures are short-lived and superficial. You know* the drugs keep you away from people and things that matter to you. Perhaps you will be able to stop using on your own and "grow out" of your dependence.

Perhaps you'll find that the support of counselling and group therapy gives you the strength to stop. Perhaps you'll try to stop again and again and keep on going *back. Your health, your home, your finances and your* relationships may slip into a state of chaos. You need a chance to put your struggle with the drugs aside, and take the time and the thought to sort out the rest of your life.

Here's where methadone maintenance treatment can help.

> *It takes some time to get a steady dose, to start working with your body, and then you'll be okay. You have to be motivated, you cannot just expect to do nothing, sit down and wait while methadone does the job for you. If you are serious about it, yes, this is the kind of break you need.*
>
> — Amir, 35
> On methadone one year

How MMT works

Methadone is a long-acting opioid drug. It fills up the same receptors in your brain as other opioid drugs and your own endorphins. While methadone can be used to relieve pain, it is most noted for its role in stabilizing the lives of people who use opioid drugs.

Methadone, through MMT, replaces the opioid drug

you've been using. When methadone is taken orally, it does not produce a high, it controls your craving for opioid drugs, and it can prevent the onset of withdrawal for 24 to 36 hours. Once you're on a stable dose of methadone, you should feel "normal," and be able to focus your life on things other than drugs.

Taking other drugs while on methadone can be both fruitless and dangerous. Because methadone is an opioid, it blocks out the effects of other opioids, preventing you from getting high. The danger here is that if you take a hit and you don't feel it, you may take more and increase the risk of overdose. (For more information on methadone and other drugs, see page 77.)

Once I went on methadone I stopped getting the cravings, whereas when I was trying to stay abstinent, I just couldn't... Since I've been on the program, I can count on my fingers how many times I've used, and that was mostly at the beginning, during the first six months, that was a real shaky time for me. And besides that, I've been slowly getting my life together. It hasn't been fast, but things are coming together.

— Marco
On methadone 15 months

The history of methadone and methadone maintenance

Methadone was first discovered in Germany before the Second World War. When the supply of morphine to Germany was cut off by the Allied forces, methadone was manufactured as a painkiller. After the war, the Americans seized the formula, and methadone was produced by drug companies.

Methadone's first role as a treatment for opioid dependence was to ease the process of withdrawal. It is still used for this today.

The potential of methadone as a maintenance treatment for opioid users was discovered during a study conducted by Drs. Marie Nyswander and Vincent P. Dole in New York in the 1960s. The study involved two people who had a chronic opioid addiction with long criminal records related to their addiction. The doctors hoped to show that when the subjects of the study were given enough drugs to satisfy their craving and keep them free of withdrawal, they would no longer commit crimes, and they'd become interested in other things.

The subjects of the study were given frequent doses of morphine to keep them comfortable. Sure enough, the subjects showed no interest in crime or other drugs.

However, other than watching a bit of TV, they showed little interest in anything. All they did all day was relax on the couch, either nodding off, or asking for their next shot.

Nyswander and Dole were ready to declare their experiment a failure. To prepare their subjects for withdrawal, they put them on methadone, intending to gradually taper down the dose. To everyone's surprise, once on methadone, the subjects perked up, showed little desire for drugs, and began to talk of other interests. One asked if he might be given some paints so that he could renew his love of painting. The other asked if he might go back to school. The doctors had found what they were looking for! With an adequate dose of methadone, their subjects were comfortable, clear-headed and able to renew their lives.

...you can't ask most drug addicts to stop and consider what vocation they want to go into, or to evaluate anything, so long as their primary preoccupation is to get drugs. When an addict no longer has to worry compulsively about his source of supply, then he can concentrate on other things. At that point, rehabilitation can become a meaningful word.

— Dr. Marie Nyswander*
Co-founder of methadone maintenance treatment

*Quoted in *A Doctor Among the Addicts* by Nat Hentoff, Rand McNally, 1968

MMT in Ontario

In 1996, there were 650 clients receiving methadone maintenance treatment in Ontario; 11 years later there were more than 17,000. This huge leap has less to do with an increase in opioid drug use in Ontario, and more to do with a current trend in public health policy. This trend aims to reduce the damage of drug use. An early sign of this trend, known as "harm reduction," was the sprouting up of neighbourhood needle exchanges aimed at controlling the spread of HIV and other infections.

Although MMT has been available in Ontario for many years, there were few doctors authorized to prescribe it, and few specialized clinics to dispense it. Even if you were an ideal candidate for methadone treatment, and you were eager to get started, it might take years before you could begin. Unable to get quick access to effective treatment, people were contracting life-threatening diseases from sharing needles, and dying from overdose at an alarming rate.

In response, changes were made to make it easier for doctors to qualify to prescribe methadone. New guidelines for the treatment of opioid-dependant patients with methadone were made available to doctors and pharmacists. More clients might now receive their treatment from their family doctor, and pick up their dose at the local pharmacy.

This increased access to methadone maintenance treatment has meant that more and more Ontario drug users have been able to leave opioid drugs like heroin and OxyContin behind, and get on with their lives.

> "Since I started on methadone, I've become a caring and involved husband, father and taxpayer. I've found my life's work, and I'm free of the crushing physical and mental burden of having to use illegal opiates. The nine months I had to wait to get on meth were torture, just torture. I was using, but I was not enjoying it. I had a real desire to change."
>
> — Jeff, 42
> On methadone six years

3 going on methadone

3 going on methadone

How to get on methadone

Depending on where you live in Ontario, you may be able to choose from a range of methadone providers, or there may be nothing available in your community. If you have not already made contact with a doctor or clinic that prescribes methadone, there are a few *different ways to find out if the treatment is available* in your area.

- See your family doctor. Tell him or her you think you're ready for methadone treatment. In order to provide MMT, your doctor must complete a training course that authorizes him or her to prescribe methadone. If your doctor does not have the authorization, and does not wish to obtain it, ask to be referred to another doctor who is authorized, or to a methadone clinic.

- If you do not have a family doctor, or if you prefer not to go that route, you may try a referral service. A number of Ontario communities offer drug and alcohol treatment assessment and referral services. To get the number of the referral service closest to you, call ConnexOntario's drug and alcohol registry of treatment at 1-800-565-8603. Their service is available 24 hours a day. When you call your local referral service, you will either be able to get an assessment and referral over the phone, or you will be able to make an appointment with a counsellor. The counsellor will then be able to direct you to a treatment that is right for you.

- All Ontario doctors who are authorized to prescribe methadone are registered with the Methadone Registry at the College of Physicians and Surgeons *of Ontario. If you are having difficulty finding a qualified doctor in your community, contact the* Methadone Registry at 416-967-2600. Let them know you are looking for methadone treatment and ask for the number of a doctor who is accepting patients in your area. Keep in mind that there are still only a limited number of doctors authorized to prescribe methadone in Ontario. If you live in a smaller community or a remote area, you may have to travel or relocate to receive treatment.

Assessment

Before you can begin taking methadone, it must be decided if the treatment is the right one for you. To make this decision, your doctor, and perhaps a nurse, counsellor, or intake worker, will need to take some time with you to get to know you. This process, called "assessment," gives your treatment providers the information they need to get you started.

The way the assessment process works varies somewhat depending on your clinic or doctor, but generally you can expect assessment to look at you as a "whole person." Assessment always includes a physical examination by a doctor and a urine test to establish that you are opioid dependent (for more on this see page 50). Assessment may also include a chest X-ray to check for tuberculosis, and, with your permission, a blood test for HIV and hepatitis. You can expect to be asked questions about your drug use, your physical and mental health, your home and family, your work, and you may be asked if you've had problems with the law.

Keep in mind that no one is judging you. Your doctor, and any others who interview you, are only interested in giving you the treatment that you have come looking for. Try to answer all questions as honestly as you can.

Assessment is also your opportunity to get to know the people who are providing the treatment. Don't be afraid to ask questions. Find out what you're being tested for. Ask what other services are available along with the methadone treatment. Gather the information you need to get ready to make decisions about your treatment.

The assessment helps to determine your course of treatment, and serves as a record of where you were when you started on methadone. Depending on your provider, you may be re-assessed again at different points in your treatment. Re-assessment lets you and your doctor know how you are progressing.

Providers differ in the amount of information they gather for assessment. You can expect assessment to take at least an hour, and possibly as much as most of a day.

The quicker you get through the assessment, the sooner it will be decided whether or not you're a candidate for methadone treatment. The time it takes to accept you as a client and begin treatment varies. In some places it may take as little as a week; in others, especially smaller cities and towns, it could take several months. If you're concerned about getting started, ask how long the process will take.

"My doctor has been exemplary in his behaviour and treatment toward me. Various other staff have been remarkably open-minded.

— Basil, 42

On methadone three years

Consent and the treatment agreement

Once you're through the tests, you've answered all the questions, and it's been decided that you're ready for methadone treatment, there are two more things:

- *Before you receive your first dose of methadone,* you must sign a consent form that allows your name to be added to the Methadone Registry database of the College of Physicians and Surgeons of Ontario. This information is kept solely to prevent clients from receiving methadone treatment from more than one doctor. Only a methadone-prescribing *doctor may confirm that you are, or are not, receiving* methadone treatment. No one else — not your employer, not the police, not welfare nor the children's aid — has access to this information.

- Many treatment providers ask clients to sign a contract, often called a "treatment agreement." This agreement states that you consent to treatment, and sets out the rules and expectations of your provider. *The treatment agreement defines policies regarding* urine samples, drug use, photo ID, carry doses, threats, violent or criminal behaviour, and the consequences if you fail to follow rules. The agreement explains that if you show up at the clinic or pharmacy stoned or drunk, you will be asked to wait or to come back later before you can receive your dose. (This is a safety precaution, because methadone mixed with other drugs can be lethal.)

The agreement should also spell out your rights, *including your right to confidentiality.*

Dose

For safety reasons, your first dose of methadone at 15 to 30 mg a day is low or moderate. The effects of methadone vary depending on individual tolerance, and *can be influenced by other drugs in your body.*

When you begin treatment you may or may not have *withdrawal symptoms for the first few days, and you* may feel drowsy and/or have drug cravings until your dose is stabilized, usually within two to six weeks. During this dose-stabilization period, you should avoid driving a car, or operating heavy machinery. See page 57 for important information on avoiding overdosing on methadone when you begin treatment.

Methadone is a slow-acting drug, which means it takes a few days to feel the full effects of an adjustment in your dose. It also means that once you are stabilized, should you miss a dose, the effects of withdrawal will come on more slowly than they do with fast-acting opioids, such as heroin.

Some clients are reluctant to increase their dose when *they first start treatment. This can result in continued drug cravings, and continued drug use. The first step of treatment is to find a dose where you can stop using* other opioids. Once you've reached that point, you can then taper down your methadone dose, if you wish.

For most people methadone works best when it's taken once a day at the same time every day. This helps to maintain a stable level of methadone in your body, keeping you feeling "normal."

It's rare, but some people metabolize methadone more quickly, and experience withdrawal well before they are due for their next dose. Usually an increase in *the daily dose will fix this problem, but in some cases* people require a "split dose," taking two half-doses 12 hours apart instead of one dose once a day. If you think you are "burning up" your methadone dose too quickly and need a split dose, ask your doctor to test the levels of methadone in your blood over the course of the day.

Methadone is safe when used properly, but it is a potent drug, and can kill. Overdoses are rare, but *the ones that do occur usually happen within the first* eight days of treatment. Generally, these deaths are the result of mixing methadone with other opioids, alcohol or downers, such as Valium. When you begin methadone treatment, be prepared to give it a chance to work for you. Stay away from other drugs — your life could depend on it.

Taking other drugs in the initial stages of your treatment also interferes with the adjustment of your dose. The symptoms you have when you begin your treatment let your doctor know how much to adjust your dose. Give it the two to six weeks it takes to get the dose at the right level for you. Hang in; it gets easier.

If you do continue to use drugs, tell your doctor or pharmacist. It could save your life. Also, let them know how you feel, if you have any cravings, or if you're feeling drowsy. They'll need this information to correct your dose.

A stable methadone dose is generally from 60 to 100 mg per day, and is adjusted according to your individual need. Never compare the amount of your dose with the amount someone else is getting. The dose that's right for you might be too much or too little for someone else. Each individual has a unique metabolism and his or her own tolerance level for the drug. Your dose is the right dose when you've reached a balance where withdrawal symptoms, drug cravings and side-effects are minimal. When your dose has been adjusted correctly, you should feel more energetic, *clear-headed, and able to fulfill your responsibilities* and pursue your interests.

In the first few weeks of treatment I felt like every nerve was on edge. I couldn't drive my car, make any decisions, I had to practice patience just to carry on a conversation. Now I have a lot more energy than I expected. I've done everything from cutting the grass to cleaning out the attic, and yesterday, I got a part-time job.

— Jill, 40
On methadone four weeks

Cost

Costs vary depending on the clinic or pharmacy. Some may charge as little as $4 for a day's dose, others as much as $15.

If you're receiving social assistance in Ontario (Ontario Works) or disability (ODSP, or Ontario Disability Support *Program), you qualify for an Ontario Drug Benefit* card, which will cover some or most of the cost of methadone. If you're not on social assistance or disability, but you have a low income, you may qualify *for the Ontario Drug Benefit Program through the*

Trillium Drug Program. Talk to your counsellor for more *information about financial help.*

Many employers now offer insurance plans that pay for prescription drugs, including methadone. If you have a health insurance plan through your work, know that no one will tell your boss, or anyone else, that the insurance company is paying for methadone for you. Some insurance companies pay the pharmacy directly, others require that you pay the pharmacy, then submit a claim to the insurance company, which then sends you a cheque. Either way no one at your work will ever be told that you ever made a claim for anything. It's *your private and personal business. It's confidential.*

For some people, there's an additional cost of methadone maintenance they may not consider. If you have to travel far to get your dose, the cost of transportation to and from the clinic or pharmacy can add up. Be prepared for this expense.

The urine sample

Like an Olympic athlete, you can expect a lot of interest in your urine. As a methadone client, samples of your urine will regularly be collected and tested for the presence of a variety of drugs, such as opioids, cocaine, marijuana, amphetamines, benzodiazepines and barbiturates. Some clinics require that you be "observed" when you are producing a urine sample. This practice is to ensure that the urine tested is yours.

Your first urine test will be part of the assessment process, when your urine will help to identify you as opioid dependent.

Once you begin methadone treatment, you will probably be asked for urine samples at least once a week for the *first eight weeks. After that, if your tests are negative* (no evidence of drug use), the frequency of these tests may decrease. After a year or so of negative tests, you may be asked for a sample only once or twice a month. Most of the time, these tests will be done at random. The frequency of urine testing may vary depending on your provider.

As well as showing if you have been using other drugs, the urine test will indicate that you have been taking your methadone. This is done as a safety precaution to ensure that your doses are being taken by you, and not by anyone else. Don't ever forget that a maintenance dose for you, may be an *overdose* for someone else. You have a tolerance for the drug because you take it every day.

Treatment providers look to the results of urine tests for signs of a continuing struggle with drug use, or as an indication of progress in treatment. For some *clients, testing negative confirms that they* can kick drugs, and gives them an extra boost of determination.

A positive urine test alerts your treatment providers to your drug use, and gives them an opportunity to protect your safety, or to offer additional emotional support. Some providers expect zero drug use, while others are more tolerant. Positive urine samples may delay or interfere with your schedule for take-home or "carry" doses, and will likely mean you'll be asked for urine samples more often.

If you test positive when you know you haven't used, you can request a retest. Sometimes labs make mistakes. It's rare, but it does sometimes happen that you could test positive for opioids after eating a poppy-seed bagel. Know that it's your responsibility to test negative, so stick to the sesame-seed variety.

Some people say, 'I would rather be out there working the street for money than to have someone watch me with my pants down peeing into a jar.' There must be a better way. It feels like discipline when you haven't done anything wrong. It's a hard one to get around. It turns people off.

— Jackie, 36
On methadone five years

Community pharmacies

More and more community pharmacies, including some big drugstore chains, are now making methadone available to clients. While doctors must be specially authorized to prescribe methadone, any pharmacy may dispense it if they choose to.

The main advantage of being able to take your methadone at a local pharmacy is convenience. You won't get the kind of support and additional services available through a methadone clinic. The degree of interest your pharmacist takes in you and your treatment may or may not extend beyond the safe administration of your dose. On the other hand, if the closest methadone clinic is miles away from home, being able to pick up your dose at your community pharmacy can make your life a whole lot easier.

For those who live in areas where there are no methadone clinics, the community pharmacy is the only way you can get MMT without having to move or spend a lot of time travelling. You'll still need to get your urine tested, but your doctor can help you to arrange to have this done at a local lab.

In cities where there are methadone clinics, some clients may prefer to pick up their dose at a pharmacy to reduce contact with other methadone clients.

When you go to the local pharmacy to collect your dose, you'll be lining up with everyone else in your neighbourhood. You may be the only one waiting for a methadone dose. If you're worried about your neighbours seeing you and knowing what you're there for, trust that the pharmacist is a professional, and will be discreet. Many pharmacies now provide a private consultation area where you can take your dose out of sight of other customers. You can also ask if you can arrange to pick up your dose at a time when the store is not busy.

If you'd like to pick up your dose at your local pharmacy, call them up or drop by and ask if they stock methadone, or if they would be willing to order it for you. Some pharmacies may be reluctant to stock methadone because they are afraid it will invite crime into their store. It's up to you and other methadone clients to prove those fears are false. Community pharmacists who dispense methadone are providing a much-needed service. Let them know you appreciate it.

If you are having trouble locating a pharmacy that will dispense methadone in your community, speak to the staff at your current pharmacy; they can help.

Confidentiality

Understanding your rights to confidentiality in treatment can make it easier to relax and open up with your doctor or counsellor. It's important that you know that no one will be told you are in treatment, or be told anything you might talk about or reveal in treatment, except in the following circumstances:

- Information about a client is often shared and discussed among members of a treatment team, such as between your doctor and counsellor.

- When you give your consent in writing. For example, if you wish to transfer to another doctor or clinic, and need to forward your records.

- If you say something, or behave in a way that makes your doctor or counsellor think that you might hurt yourself or someone else, the law states that he or she must inform others in order to provide safety and protect lives. Incidents or suspicion of child neglect or abuse must be reported to the police or child protection agency.

- If you are facing trial and the court subpoenas your treatment records as evidence.

If your treatment is a condition imposed by the drug courts, probation or parole, or is a condition of keeping the custody of your child, you may be asked to sign a *form that waives some of your rights to confidentiality.*

All testing for HIV and other communicable diseases *is confidential. If you test positive, however, this* information will be shared with public health, and your needle-sharing or sexual partners must be informed that they have been exposed to the disease. You will have a chance to ask any questions you may have about this when you are tested.

Make a point of discussing the limits of confidentiality with your doctor or counsellor early in treatment. This is especially important if you have children. When *children are involved, your right to confidentiality may* be waived if the children are deemed to be "at risk." This term is open to some individual interpretation. Some treatment providers may think that any evidence of illicit drug use puts children at risk. You'll feel a lot more comfortable if you understand your treatment *providers' definition of the term.*

As mentioned earlier, all methadone clients are registered with the Methadone Registry of the College of Physicians and Surgeons of Ontario (CPSO). This information is available to no one other than a methadone-prescribing doctor, and is kept only to ensure that no one receives treatment from more than one doctor. The only information collected is your name, date of birth, gender, health card number, city of residence when entering treatment, and who you are receiving treatment from (name of doctor and/or associated clinic). If you change treatment providers, or if you leave treatment, you will be asked to sign a form that allows the CPSO to change the information about you in their database.

A Patient's Guide — Avoiding Overdose in the First Two Weeks of Methadone Treatment*

Methadone is a very safe drug, but accidental overdoses *sometimes happen in the first two weeks of treatment.* The questions and answers below will help you get through this period safely. Share this information sheet with a friend or family member.

Why can't my doctor increase my dose more quickly?

When you first start methadone, you want to get on the right dose as soon as possible. But your doctor has to increase your dose slowly over several weeks, because your body takes time to adjust to methadone, and (unlike other narcotics), methadone builds up slowly in your bloodstream over several days. A dose that may feel like too little on a Monday could put you in hospital by Thursday.

What can I take to relieve withdrawal and help me sleep until the methadone begins to work?

Only take medications that are prescribed by your methadone doctor. If you're on a medication prescribed by another doctor, your methadone doctor needs to approve it because it could interact with methadone. Substances that make you relaxed or sleepy can be dangerous. This includes alcohol, opioids, benzodiazepines (Ativan, Valium, Rivotril, etc.), antihistamines such as Gravol or Benadryl, and certain types of antidepressants and tranquilizers. Even certain antibiotics can be dangerous, by blocking the breakdown of methadone in the body. So make sure to check all medications with your methadone physician.

Isn't methadone supposed to make you sleepy?

No. You are supposed to feel normal on methadone, not high or sleepy. Methadone builds up so slowly that someone can feel a bit sleepy during the day, lie down for a nap and not wake up. So please take the following precautions:

- Only take your methadone in the morning.
- *See your doctor twice a week for the first two weeks.*
- Discuss your methadone treatment with a close friend or family member. If they see that you're drowsy, they must call your methadone doctor or an ambulance.

What are some of the symptoms if my methadone dose is too high?

- You may feel sleepy, and nod off several times during the day.
- You may be forgetful.
- *You may be difficult to wake up from your sleep.*
- You may experience slurred speech, stumbling walk, or appear drunk.

If these things are occurring you must call your doctor immediately or go to Emergency as you may be overdosing.

I've been offered a small amount of methadone by a methadone patient at the pharmacy. This can't hurt — I know I need 80 mg!

Above all, don't take any extra methadone. It's probably safe for your friend, but could be lethal for you. You took 80 mg *once* and were okay. If you had taken 80 mg every day for three or four days, you might have died. *Remember, it takes five days for a certain dose to build* up in your blood.

*Reproduced with permission from *Methadone Maintenance Guidelines*, November 2005. Copyright 2005, The College of Physicians and Surgeons of Ontario.

4

living with methadone

4 living with methadone

Carry doses

For the first two months of treatment, you will be expected to go to the clinic or pharmacy daily to drink your dose under observation. The daily contact during this initial period helps the staff to see how the treatment is working for you. They'll be looking to see if your dose is enough or too much, if you are experiencing side-effects, and if you are using other drugs. After two months, you may be able to begin to take home, or "carry," doses.

Carry doses are a privilege given to you when you have progressed well in treatment, and are prepared to take responsibility for using and storing the doses safely. Some providers grant carry privileges only to those who produce drug-free urines.

You will likely be asked to sign an agreement stating that you take responsibility for the safe and secure storage of carry doses, and that you understand that the doses are to be taken by you and only you. Your carry privileges may be taken away if you fail to meet the terms of agreement, or if your urine tests positive for drug use.

Before you begin to carry doses, you must agree to bring any empty or full dose bottles back to the clinic or pharmacy at any time, if requested. You must also agree to provide a urine sample upon request. Giving away or selling carry doses may result in criminal charges being laid against you, and in the suspension of your carry privileges.

You must come to the clinic or pharmacy to collect your carry doses. Home delivery is not available.

Some clinics or pharmacies require that you return all carry dose bottles once they are empty.

Safety and storage

Your maintenance dose of methadone could seriously harm or kill someone who has no tolerance for the drug. A small child might mistake your dose for ordinary juice, drink it, and die. Never transfer your dose to a container that might make it easier to mistake what's inside. This has led to tragedy in the past. You are responsible for the safekeeping of your doses, and you will be held responsible if someone else drinks your dose.

Even though carry doses are generally stored in childproof bottles, you are strongly urged to keep *your doses in a locked box, such as one sold for fishing* tackle or cash.

It's recommended that you keep your carries in the *fridge, but some clients find that the juice mix used to* dilute your dose keeps well at room temperature.

Schedule

The length of time it takes for you to begin to carry doses may vary depending on your provider. Also, the number of doses you are given at any time may vary depending on your provider. Whether or not you have been using illicit drugs will be considered, as will the safety and stability of your home. Ask to *find out when and under what conditions you will* be given carry doses.

Lost or stolen doses

Carry doses that are lost or stolen may not be replaced, and must be reported to police in order to alert the public and prevent harm. Loss or theft of carry doses may result in having your carry privileges suspended, meaning you will have to report to the clinic or pharmacy every day to collect your dose. It is your responsibility to store your carry doses safely.

When you can't get to the clinic or pharmacy

It's important that you don't miss your dose even if you can't make it to the clinic or pharmacy. Your treatment need not be interrupted even in the following situations:

- You wish to travel away from home.
- You are ill.
- You are in an accident.
- You are hospitalized.
- You are arrested.

In general, follow these guidelines to help ensure you don't miss your dose:

- Some clinics will issue you a methadone client photo ID card. If you have one, carry it with you at all times to identify you as a client.

- Keep the phone number of your clinic or pharmacy and doctor in your wallet. If you are hospitalized or arrested, contacting your pharmacy or doctor will ensure that you receive the correct dose.

- Talk to your doctor about getting a Medic Alert bracelet stating that you are a methadone client, and wear the bracelet at all times. If you are in an accident, this will ensure you get the correct medication.

Going out of town / out of Canada

It takes a little organization and thinking ahead, but if you want to travel, you can go a long way, and still get your methadone. You may be able to "guest dose" at another pharmacy, in another town or city, in another province, or even in another country. When planning a trip, talk to your doctor well in advance for help in making the arrangements for guest dosing.

If you have earned carry privileges, and you wish to take a short trip outside Canada, you may want to carry your doses across the border. Many people do travel with carries, and have no problem with border guards. You should know, though, that carrying methadone across the border into some countries is, by the books, against the law, although the law is not enforced. If you're travelling to the States, for example, and you want to take your carries with you, it can be done, it is done, and U.S. customs will even tell *you that you can do it, but officially it's not legal.*

When crossing any border, it's always wise to treat the guards with polite respect, and not draw attention to yourself. Don't try to hide your methadone; if they *find it hidden they'll get upset. If they ask, show it to* them. It's a legally obtained prescription drug. It's your medication.

Here are some guidelines from U.S. customs for taking methadone across the border:

- Be sure the bottles containing your doses are marked by the pharmacy with your name and the prescription information.

- Carry only the doses you will need for personal use while you are in the U.S.

- Travel with a letter from your doctor or clinic that describes your treatment and your dose. Be sure the *letter includes a telephone number to call to confirm* the letter.

Methadone is available as a prescription drug in many countries around the world. The INDRO Web site (http://indro-online.de/travel.htm) has information on methadone travel regulations for over 150 countries. The site includes, for some countries, names of methadone providers, and customs contacts. Follow up to be sure the information is up to date. If you don't have access to the Web, your pharmacist should be *able to find out about the legal status and availability* of methadone in the country that you wish to visit.

Illness

Methadone can only be administered by qualified medical personnel. Even if you qualify for carry doses, you cannot arrange to have them delivered to your home. If you are too ill to get to the pharmacy to collect your dose, contact your pharmacy to let them know. In extreme situations your pharmacist may be willing to deliver your dose and watch you take it.

Hospital

If you are admitted to hospital, either as a planned visit, or in an emergency situation, it's extremely important that the staff there know that you are a methadone client. This is important not only so that you can receive your dose, but also because there are other drugs that can be dangerous if taken in combination with methadone. Encourage the hospital staff to speak with your doctor about your medication, and your care.

I was taken in to emergency, and when I told them I was on methadone, I thought, oh my God, I'm going to have one hell of a time getting this, and it was so quickly set up, I had my dose exactly when I needed it. You need to contact your doctor, of course, and it might depend on what hospital you're going to, but for me it was no problem.

— Jackie, 36
On methadone five years

Arrest / jail

If you have to spend time in a provincial or federal jail in Ontario, you should be able to continue your treatment while in jail. Both the provincial and federal governments are striving to provide methadone treatment to anyone who was receiving treatment immediately or soon before arrest or the beginning of a sentence. If you have any problems with receiving treatment, be sure to contact your methadone doctor or clinic for help in advocating for you. Doctors serving jail populations in Ontario are either authorized to prescribe methadone, or are able to arrange that it be made available. At the present time, you may continue, but not begin, methadone treatment while in jail.

Dealing with side-effects

Constipation

Like other opioid drugs, methadone can cause constipation. The best way to treat this annoying *complaint is with foods that are high in fibre. Stock up* on bran cereal, whole-wheat bread, brown rice, fresh fruits and vegetables. Canned beans are loaded with *fibre. Prunes and prune juice are a good old-fashioned* tried-and-true remedy. Wash it all through with plenty of water.

Beware of foods that are high in fat like cheese and pastries. These are harder to digest and tend to make your system sluggish.

If you're not used to a high-fibre diet, go easy at first. These foods can cause bloating and gas. Gradually your body will be able to process this diet, without too much embarrassment.

Avoid treating ongoing constipation with laxatives. These drugs interfere with the absorption of nutrients in your body. They are only meant for occasional use. If *the high-fibre diet is not enough, or if you don't think you can stand another bite of bran, fibre supplements* are available at pharmacies. These contain psyllium, which are the seeds of a banana-like plant. These must be taken with a lot of water. They are perfectly safe, and should provide relief.

And finally, exercise can help. You might prefer something vigorous like running or dancing, but if you don't, even a relaxed stroll after a meal or tossing the Frisbee in the park can keep things moving. The point is to keep active.

Excessive sweating

This persistent symptom can be difficult to control. Sometimes, if you are on a high dose, lowering the dose may stop the sweating, although some people continue to experience this side-effect even on a low dose. If a higher dose is what you need to stay comfortable in other ways, or if lowering your dose doesn't help, you may need to learn to live with *the sweating. Lighter, natural-fibre clothes, strong* antiperspirant and baby powder helps some to feel less humid.

Changes in sex drive

Some people on methadone say they have little sex drive, and are unable to experience an orgasm. Others say that since they are off other opioids and feeling better, their sex life has improved. It's an individual experience. In some cases, you may be taking another medication that's affecting your sex drive. If you are having problems of a sexual nature, your doctor may be able to offer some good advice.

Methadone and employment

Once you're on a stable dose, the fact that you take methadone shouldn't affect your choice of work, or how well you do your job. For most jobs, there's no reason to mention that you take methadone, and your employer has no right to know. If you wish to do a job that involves operating a vehicle, however, your doctor must be willing to "recommend" you for a license. Methadone clients applying for a commercial license are considered on a case-by-case basis, and must prove that they are stable, and show no other drug use on their urine test.

HIV, hepatitis C and methadone

Methadone can be a great benefit to opioid users who are HIV or hepatitis C (HCV) positive. Because methadone allows you to lead a "normal" life, it's easier to take care of yourself, to eat better, and to take your medications at the right times. Methadone helps you to feel well, and to be able to do the things you want to do with your life.

Be sure to discuss any prescription drugs you are taking with your methadone doctor. Some of these drugs may interfere with methadone, and your dose may need to be adjusted.

Resolving treatment problems

If you are unhappy with your treatment, your first approach should be to talk it over. If, for example, you feel your dose has not been adjusted correctly, talk to your doctor, explain what you feel. That might be all it *takes to fix the problem.*

If you feel there's a problem with your treatment that *hasn't been fixed by talking to your doctor or your* counsellor, you may consider changing your provider. If you live in the Toronto area, there are a number of doctors and clinics to choose from. You should be able *to find one whose approach to treatment meets your* needs. If you live in a smaller community, you might have to work it out. There may only be one doctor who can prescribe methadone where you live.

As a last resort, and if you feel the problems with your treatment provider are severe and remain unresolved, you can complain to the College of Physicians and Surgeons of Ontario at 416-967-2600.

Most of the professionals you'll meet through treatment will treat you with respect, and offer support and encouragement. Be good to them, and nine times out of ten, they'll be good to you.

> *Talk to your doctor, tell him or her everything that you're feeling, be open and honest. It's so important that you build a relationship based on trust.*
>
> — Beth, 39
> On methadone four years

"I object to being made to wait so long to see my doctor. I usually have to wait from 15 to 45 minutes to be seen. If this were an occasional thing, it wouldn't be so bad, but I have to see my doctor very frequently. It makes me late for work. I think that if an addict like me can be on time, then surely a professional doctor can be on time."

— Chris, 49
On methadone 17 years

"I love the staff here. It's not easy to deal with angry and distrusting addicts. They fought for me when I didn't think I was worth fighting for."

— Sharon, 46
On methadone four years

"Always treat staff with respect, regardless of the circumstances or your mood. Be assertive, not aggressive. Don't whine. Don't complain to the staff about another staff member. If you don't behave like a model client, all you get is medicated, nothing more, nothing less."

— Janet, 26
On methadone four years

I am constantly amazed that after I have a blow out, i.e., I freak out at clinic staff, they are always very nice to me like nothing ever happened. I really really appreciate that because I feel badly enough that I was rude to them in the first place.

    — Bonnee, 43
       On methadone two years

Clinics vary. I've been to a few different places. At one place, the doctors, pharmacist, etc., were all exploitive and clueless. At another everyone was very cold, there was no support. Where I am now is amazing, all the staff, including my counsellor, are superb.

    — Spacey, 30
       On methadone six years

Changing methadone providers

If you move to a different neighbourhood or town, or if you do decide you want to try another doctor or clinic, you can change your methadone provider. All that it takes, once you identify where you want to go and they've agreed to take you, is for you to give permission to have your records transferred. There will be a form to sign. Ask how long the process will take.

Involuntary discharge

All methadone treatment providers have some rules, and some are stricter than others in how they deal with a client who breaks the rules. Understand that, depending on the rules of your treatment provider, you may be discharged from treatment if you do any of the following:

- behave in a threatening, violent or disruptive manner toward staff, other clients or other people

- sell or give away your methadone

- don't show up to pick up your dose more than three days in a row, or miss picking up your dose often (without good reason)

- commit an illegal act on the premises, such as shoplifting or selling drugs

- continue to use other drugs

- fail to attend group therapy sessions.

Some providers may taper down your dose before you are cut off, and some may help you to organize a transfer to another program. Some may accept you back at a later date. Incidents of violent or other criminal behaviour can result in an abrupt end to treatment. How involuntary discharge is handled is entirely at the discretion of the clinic or pharmacy.

5
methadone and other drugs

5 methadone and other drugs

Methadone and pain relief

Methadone can provide effective pain relief, but when it is used for pain, the dosage is different from the dosage used to treat opioid dependence. Pain in methadone clients is sometimes under-medicated because medical staff may assume that the methadone you take provides pain relief. The truth is, once you are on a stable dose of methadone, you may be tolerant to its pain-relieving effects. This means that if you are in pain, you need pain medication just as much as anyone else in a similar situation.

For example, if you have a headache, menstrual cramps or any other low-level pain, you should get relief with a normal dose of aspirin or Tylenol without codeine. If you require surgery, or are in an accident, you should continue to take your normal dose of methadone, and receive pain medication for the same length of time as anyone else in a similar condition.

In some cases, if you are tolerant to the pain-relieving effects of methadone, you may also be tolerant to the pain-relieving effects of other opioids. Some clients run into trouble with this because the medical staff who are treating them may suspect they are complaining of pain in order to get more drugs to get high.

If you are booked for surgery or dental work, ask your methadone doctor to provide you with a letter that says you are on methadone and how that affects your needs for pain relief. A better option is to ask the doctor or dentist who is treating you to talk to your methadone doctor.

When you are struggling to overcome drug dependence, you may question whether or not you want or need to take medication for pain relief. Some may fear that even taking an aspirin might lead them back into taking other drugs. Others may feel that their history *of opioid use makes it even more difficult for them to* cope with pain. If pain is a problem for you, talk to your doctor.

Double doctoring

Any time you are given a prescription for "narcotic" drugs by more than one doctor, you must report it to the other doctor. In Canada, narcotic drugs such as Tylenol 3, Percocet or methadone are "controlled substances." It is against the law for you to receive a prescription for these drugs from more than one doctor, without them both knowing. It's your responsibility to let your doctor know. If you don't, you could be accused of "double doctoring," which is against the law.

Mixing methadone with other drugs

Methadone is a potent drug, and can interact with other drugs to have undesirable or dangerous effects. Your doctor knows not to prescribe drugs that will interact or interfere with methadone, but it's up to you to know the potential impact of any recreational drugs you might take.

Dangerous combinations include:

Alcohol and Valium

Mixing methadone with alcohol or Valium can kill you. *The danger is particularly high when you first start* treatment. Most methadone-related deaths involve alcohol and other drugs, and occur early in treatment.

Alcohol, Valium (or other benzodiazepine drugs, such as Ativan, Xanax, Restoril and clonazepam) and methadone are all central nervous system (CNS) depressants. If you take too much of any

CNS depressant, it slows down your breathing, which can lead to heart failure and even death.

When you mix CNS depressants together, they intensify each other's effects. This means they can make you feel more drunk or stoned than you might expect. It also means that the effect on your *breathing is intensified. Combining these drugs is* extremely dangerous.

If you show up at your clinic or pharmacy, and it's clear that you've been drinking or using other drugs, you won't be given your methadone dose until the pharmacist is convinced that it's safe. Some pharmacists might ask you to do a breathalyzer test if they suspect you've been drinking. It's their job to medicate you safely. They're on your side.

When you're under the influence of alcohol or Valium, your judgment is clouded. It's easier to get into a situation where you might think you can use your drug of choice "just one more time," or, just as serious, you might think the person who's offering it to you is a friend who's doing you a favour. If you want to keep control of your actions, and protect yourself from people you can't trust, make it easier for yourself: keep your head clear.

Alcohol can also have the effect of speeding up the metabolism of methadone in your body. This means that the methadone will wear off quicker, and you might end up feeling sick before it's time to get your next dose.

Is there a safe level of drinking?

If you want to drink, this is a question you should ask your doctor. Whether or not it's safe for you to have a drink or two now and then depends on a number of factors. For example, anyone who is hepatitis C positive should avoid drinking altogether because of the stress alcohol puts on the liver. Another consideration is how alcohol might interact with any other medications you might be taking besides methadone.

Even though alcohol is everywhere and it's cheap and it's legal, when you're on methadone, drinking can cause more problems than it's worth.

Other opioids

Methadone is an opioid drug, and will block the high of other opioid drugs, such as heroin, codeine, OxyContin and Percocet. That means that if you're on methadone, and, for example, you take some heroin, you might not feel much of anything. If you take more heroin, you could be in trouble. Just because you don't feel the high doesn't mean the drug is not affecting your body. You can still overdose.

Since I started on methadone, I've stopped using other opiates. Now I can keep friends.

— Don, 39

On methadone four months

Drugs that will cause withdrawal

Drugs that reverse the effects of opioids and cause you to go into withdrawal are called "opioid antagonists."

The opioid antagonist you'd be given if you overdosed, and got to the hospital in time, is called naloxone. Another one you may hear of is naltrexone, which is prescribed for the treatment of opioid or alcohol dependence.

While you're not likely to take either of those drugs if you're looking to get high, there are some drugs whose effects are similar to an opioid high, but will also cause withdrawal. An example of this is Talwin, which is what pharmacists call an opioid agonist/antagonist. That means it produces some of the same effects as opioids, such as pain relief, but will also cause you to go into withdrawal if you have opioids, such as methadone, in your system. On the street Talwin is a main ingredient of "Ts and Rs." Don't take it. You'll get sick.

Cocaine and crack

Coke is a highly addictive drug that can make you anxious and paranoid, even violent and deluded. Too many people who get on methadone start using coke or crack to replace opioids. If you do that, you'll have a new set of problems, and methadone can't help you to deal with a cocaine addiction.

Marijuana

Having a few tokes may be safer than having a few drinks, or smoking crack, but like any drug, marijuana can have negative effects, and it can be misused. Some people dismiss the risks of using grass, saying it helps them to relax or improves their appetite. While marijuana may have these effects, it can also distort your senses and make it harder to think clearly. In some people, THC can induce anxiety and depression.

It may seem obvious, but the reality is, marijuana is illegal, it's habit forming, and if you smoke too much, it can reduce your motivation. Keep in mind too that if your methadone provider has a low tolerance for drug use, and you smoke marijuana, it could show up in your urine tests for up to a month, depending on how much you smoke.

Other drugs / vitamins / herbal remedies

Some other drugs, including those you get from your pharmacist, can be dangerous if taken in combination with methadone. Others may alter or interfere with the effectiveness of methadone. To be safe, and to be sure you're comfortable, let your pharmacist know about all other drugs you take.

A part of me wishes I hadn't gone on meth because it has an intense withdrawal and is just as hard to get off of as junk. On the other hand, meth has saved my life, I think, because if I hadn't gone on, I'd probably be dead by now. Since I started on meth I've stopped using drugs and I've got my life on track in a good way.

For meth to work you've got to be strong. You can't let yourself take a little something if you're feeling sick. You've got to keep busy. Stay away from the people you used to get high with. Stay away from the places that bring back memories, and make you want to get high again. You've really got to want to get off drugs.

— Harvey, 37
On methadone five years

Safe injection

Everybody's hoping that once you're on methadone, you'll never touch another needle in your life. Sometimes, though, it takes longer to get clear of drugs than it does to begin methadone treatment. Always avoid injecting, but if you do, please follow this advice:

Always use a new needle. Even cleaning with bleach may not protect you from becoming infected with hepatitis C (HCV). Many, maybe even most, injection drug users are infected with HCV. Sharing needles also puts you at high risk of becoming infected with HIV, or of passing it on to someone else. Needles are one thing you should never share. Besides, they are only meant to be used once. After that they are dull, and could damage your veins. Dispose of used needles safely so no one gets sick or hurt. Needles are available through needle exchanges, pharmacies and public health departments.

6 counselling and other services

6 counselling and other services

Counselling services

All methadone clients are encouraged to combine methadone treatment with counselling. Some people *benefit enormously from the support, encouragement* and guidance they get from counselling. It is generally accepted that methadone treatment with counselling is far more effective than methadone treatment alone.

The level of counselling services that are available through your methadone treatment can vary widely depending on your treatment provider. Some providers make counselling or group therapy participation a condition of receiving methadone. Others may or may not provide counselling, and leave it up to clients to decide whether or not they wish to seek out counselling services.

Counselling may be supplied by a drug treatment counsellor or a social worker, or you may be counselled by your doctor. The level of training and expertise of counsellors can vary widely, from those who can tell *you where to find food banks and hostels, to those* who are able to treat complex psychological problems. Be sure to discuss your counselling needs with your treatment provider to see if you need a referral to outside services.

Other services available in conjunction with your methadone treatment vary depending on where you go:

- If you have your methadone prescribed by your doctor and go to your local pharmacy to take your dose, services in addition to medical counselling will depend on your doctor.

- Methadone clinics offer a variety of additional services. Counselling services are standard. Other services may include advocacy on your behalf with welfare and children's aid, legal, medical and dentistry services, housing services and needle exchange. Some clinics provide a resource area or a community space for clients to drop in and spend time.

- Many short- or long-term residential treatment centres and therapeutic communities are abstinence-based, but more and more are accepting residents in methadone treatment. The services offered by these facilities vary depending on the program.

The benefits of counselling

It's accepted wisdom that talking out your problems with someone you trust can help to make things clearer, simpler and easier to solve.

Most often the person you trust is a friend or family member. This is the person you call when you want help or advice. This is the person who listens. If you have someone like this in your life, someone who can offer you support, you may be more fortunate than you know. Strong personal relationships give emotional strength, and you need that strength to learn to live without drugs.

Even if you have a good friend, it is still a good idea *to seek out the services of a qualified counsellor.* Your friend may be wise in many ways, but he or she may not know how to help you in your struggle with drugs. Sometimes your friend may be too close and too involved to be able to see clearly. You need someone from outside, someone who can listen and give you *back a clear reflection of what's really going on.* Find a counsellor with experience in helping people in your situation.

Having the services of a good counsellor can also help to ensure that you keep your good friend. If you're *trying to get through a difficult time in your life, you* may be looking to your friend for help a little too often. You may not be able to offer much in return. You can avoid stressing your relationship by laying the heavy stuff on your counsellor. Your counsellor's job is to listen, to understand, and to help you learn how to solve your problems for yourself.

Talking to your counsellor

You may find it difficult to open up and trust your counsellor at first. He or she understands that, and is willing to help you at whatever level you need. *To begin with, you might need help to find a better* place to live, to get a job, to get through court, to get your kids back, or to get into school. When you're ready, you'll be encouraged to talk about your drug use.

As you progress in counselling, you should find it easier to relax and open up. Your counsellor is not going to judge you for what you have or haven't done. Your counsellor's job is to understand and, more importantly, to help *you* understand why you use drugs. You'll talk about what will happen if you continue to use, and what will happen if you stop. You'll talk about taking responsibility for your drug use, and for the things you may have done to get the money to pay for drugs. You'll talk about making a future plan.

Counselling is sometimes optional, but the success of your treatment may depend on it.

My counsellor has been a solid force in trying to get to the bottom of my using. She never gives up on me. She makes me feel worthwhile, and her confidence in me really helps.

    — Bonnee, 43
      On methadone two years

Talk to your doctor and therapist. Don't listen to what you hear from other clients. The staff is understanding of the pressures and problems you have, and are always there to listen. The counselling programs are very helpful.
   Take it one day at a time.

    — Jalima, 30
      On methadone three years

I changed counsellors because the one I had was inexperienced with drug problems. I had to seek out professional therapeutic help. I found someone who is empathetic and good, whom I continue to see regularly. After a few months of coming to him I was able to see the root of my problems. I'd needed that insight for 10 years.

    — Janet, 26
      On methadone four years

Group therapy

In addition to individual counselling, you may want participate in group therapy. This usually involves sharing your experiences with others who are seeking help for problems similar to your own. Some methadone providers require that you participate in group therapy in order to receive treatment.

Family therapy

Depending on your situation, involving your family in counselling can be very helpful in overcoming a drug problem. Your family needs to understand why you use drugs and how they can help you to stop using. Family therapy can also help you to understand the other members of your family, and what support you can expect from them.

Methadone Anonymous

Methadone Anonymous is based on the same 12-step program and meeting format as Narcotics Anonymous and Alcoholics Anonymous. The emphasis of all the 12-step programs is on achieving a desire to stop using drugs, spiritual growth, honesty and helping others help themselves.

At an MA meeting, all members are methadone clients. Talking with others who are dealing with their drug dependence in the same way can offer an understanding that may not be available from family and friends. Meetings include the opportunity to share experiences with other group members.

MA groups are still rare in Ontario. To find out if there is an MA group in your community, check with your doctor or counsellor. For more information, check out Methadone Anonymous on the web at http://www. methadone-anonymous.org.

"*I never feel like going out to the meetings, but when I get there I'm always glad I came. Sometimes, you know, my wife doesn't understand, so it's good to talk with other addicts. The group helps each other. It works for me, I've been off drugs now for three years, and I tell ya, the only time I stayed straight before was when I was in jail. When I was out, I'd take maybe 70 Tylenol 3 and 10 Percodans a day, plus, I was a drunk. A skid row drunk. I'm straight now because of the meetings. It works for me, and it could work for anybody.*"

— Dan, 45

On methadone four years

Learning to live without drugs

Few people can stop using drugs overnight just because they decide they want to quit. For most, it is an ongoing process that takes time, patience and determination. You may have to learn a whole new way of living.

Say, for example, you wanted to learn to play the guitar. You know you'd have to practise many, many hours before you were any good. You'd have to learn the chords and listen to the great players. A good teacher could really help. As you got better, there *would be moments of reward, like when a difficult* chord change got easier, and sounded so good. If you already play guitar, or any instrument, or if you do any sport, or art, you know what it took to get you to be as good as you are. You know what it will take to get better.

Becoming great at anything takes time, patience and determination. You can become great at *not* using drugs. Make your decision and follow through. Don't be afraid to ask for help when you need it. The more you practise living without drugs, the better you'll get at it. Someday it will just be a part of what you are and what you do, like playing guitar or cooking supper or driving a car. You won't need help any more. You may even be able to offer help to others. It *will* get easier.

"For me the 'harm reduction' approach really worked. I could continue to use until I was ready to quit, and could stay on the program. I used heroin for 29 years. I've been clean for four-and-a-half years. I now have a future to work towards. I no longer have the fear that I could die any time, any where, any day – alone. I have my life back.

My advice to those coming onto methadone is this: If you fail, don't punish yourself, just try again."

    — Sharon, 46
      On methadone five years

"The biggest problem people face is not actually the drugs themselves, but trying to find ways to spend time. By the time people go on methadone, they've lost their friends and the only people they have left are their "drug buddies," and they don't want to hang out with them. So they are alone trying to find ways to have fun but they are so used to their routine that they are now trying to stay away from that they have no idea of things to do."

    — Laura, 22
      On methadone one year

What'll I do if I don't do drugs?

Doing drugs can fill up your day. It's a busy life: getting the cash, finding your dealer and getting high. Drugs can be a reason to get up and go out. They can offer an identity, a lifestyle, a career. Drugs can block out the past, and stand in the way of planning for what's ahead. When you go on methadone and you stop doing other drugs, the days will open up. You'll be able to choose from a variety of possibilities of what you might do with your time. Drugs won't decide it for you.

The surprising thing is, this newfound freedom can be *hard to adjust to. For some, the time is easily filled* and welcome. This may be the chance to get back to school or to get ahead in your work. If you have small *children, your days can fly by taking care of them. Others may need to search harder to fill the gap that* drugs have left. You need to learn new ways to spend your day. If your day is empty, you may think you're bored, and that drugs would make your life more interesting. When you learn to jump over that trap, your life becomes more your own.

Having things you want to do with your time, that you enjoy, that you take pride in, and that make you feel good about yourself can be a great motivator to staying off drugs. Getting out to get your methadone takes up a chunk of the day, but it still gives you plenty of time to get into something else. If it seems like everyone else is busy and you're left with nothing to do, take that time to work out what you *want* to do. Talk it over with your family, your friends, your counsellor. And while you're thinking about it, keep busy. Don't give yourself time to get high. Be creative, be productive. Fill up your life with things you love that can love you back, and make no time for drugs.

Got a job, went back to school, got a better job. You've got to quit the life, not just the dope. Maintenance allows you to adjust slowly to life without heroin, and eventually drugs. My life is normal now. I only have boredom to fight.

— Spacey, 30
On methadone six years

Channel the energy you used to use to support your habit into positive things. If you're at all religious, even if you never thought of it while addicted, open yourself to spiritual ways. It's the most powerful source of strength that's out there, and it's free.

— Janet, 26
On methadone four years

7
women, family and methadone

7 women, family and methadone

Birth control

If you've been using heroin, OxyContin or other opioids, you may have stopped having your period, and think that you can't get pregnant. Then again, if you've stopped having your period, you may be pregnant. If you're not sure, get a pregnancy test from a doctor, pharmacist or community health centre.

If you're not pregnant, and you are sexually active, use birth control. If you begin to use less opioids, or if you begin to take methadone, your period will likely start up again, and your chances of getting pregnant will increase. Use birth control. It's best if you wait until you're ready to give up drugs entirely before you get pregnant.

Pregnancy

If you are pregnant, and you are still using opioids, call your doctor and ask to begin methadone maintenance as soon as possible. The short cycle of the high and the recurring threshold of withdrawal is the most immediate threat to your baby. Withdrawal causes the uterus to contract, and may bring on miscarriage or premature birth. Methadone maintenance is safe for the baby, it keeps you free of withdrawal, and gives you a chance to take care of yourself.

If you are pregnant, you may want to take a good look at your options. If you think you want to keep your baby, consider how you'll live, what support you'll have and if you're ready for the responsibility. Another option is to carry the baby through pregnancy, and offer it for adoption. Healthy babies are in high demand. Another option is abortion. Keep in mind that if you decide to terminate the pregnancy, it is safest *and easiest in the first 12 weeks of pregancy. If you put* off the decision, you will no longer have the choice.

Pregnant women beginning methadone maintenance are encouraged to stay in hospital while making the change from their opioid of choice to methadone. This usually takes a few days, but may be less, or may be more.

Once on methadone, you should feel relief from
the physical drug cravings. You'll be more likely
to eat better, smoke less or not at all, and avoid
alcohol and other drugs. You can be like any other
pregnant woman, enjoy the extra attention,
and prepare to welcome the new life you
have begun.

If you plan to keep your baby once it is born, you may
be asked to reassure the children's aid that you have
stopped using drugs, and are settled and ready to be a
mother. Look to your doctor and counsellor for help in
dealing with the children's aid.

" *When I found out I was pregnant, I was convinced, and
everyone else was convinced, I could not get clean and take
care of myself and have the baby. The doctor said to me, 'You
can do this,' and he made me believe that I could.*

*I was worried that the baby would have withdrawals
when she was born, but all she had were some tremors. I
held her and she was okay. I breastfed her and that was
great, no problems. They kept her in the hospital for five days
and I stayed with her. When the children's aid came in to the
hospital and saw how I'd bonded with the baby, they backed
off and closed my file.*

*She's two years old now and she's fantastic. I was
scared and worried what the methadone might do to her,
but she's just fine: she started walking at only nine months,*

and she's smart. The pregnancy happened at just the right time, it saved me from the whole addiction thing, it showed me what I could do.

— Roxanne, 26
On methadone three years

Infant withdrawal

Some babies born to mothers on methadone will go through withdrawal after birth. This usually begins a few days after birth, but symptoms could arise two to four weeks after birth and may last several weeks or months. Infants in withdrawal may be cranky, not eat or sleep well, or have a fever, vomiting, trembling and occasionally seizures. Infants going through withdrawal must be closely watched in hospital, depending on how well the baby is doing. If the symptoms are severe, your baby may be medicated to ease the withdrawal. *Never* give methadone to your baby. Even a small amount can be enough to kill a baby. Let your doctor manage the baby's withdrawal.

While it is not known for certain what long-term effects the exposure to methadone may have on your baby, babies born to mothers on methadone usually do as well as other babies, and have a much greater chance at doing well than babies born to mothers on heroin or other opioids. Taking methadone while pregnant will not result in any deformities or disease in the baby.

Breastfeeding

Women on low doses of methadone who are not HIV positive are encouraged to breastfeed. Women who are hepatitis C positive are usually able to breastfeed, but should check with their doctor.

The benefits of breastfeeding are felt to outweigh the effect of the tiny amount of methadone that enters the breast milk. Once the baby is three to six months old, and is drinking large amounts of breast milk, he or she is also getting larger amounts of methadone. For this reason the baby should either be weaned at this time, or the mother should stop taking methadone. (Mothers should only stop methadone if they are sure this will not lead to a return to drug use.) If you feel that you want to wean your baby because of methadone exposure, talk to your doctor. Your doctor should be able to give you advice about when you should begin *weaning and about the risks and benefits of continuing* to breastfeed.

Child protection services

Taking care of kids can be a tough job even when everything is going well, and when things are rough, it can be overwhelming. Every mother needs support, but not every mother gets as much support as she needs. Ideally, the role of your children's aid society (CAS) is to give you a hand when you need help caring for your child, and to provide access to training in parenting skills. If you are having trouble coping with parenthood on top of other struggles, talk to your counsellor about it. You may need the support of the CAS.

Most CAS caseworkers are more interested in seeing *your child enjoy and benefit from your care than in* taking him or her away from you. They want to see you provide a healthy, loving and secure home for your child. Unfortunately, not all caseworkers are well informed about methadone treatment. They may make assumptions about you based on your history of drug use. Dealing with the CAS can be confusing. Again, look to your doctor or counsellor for help.

In some communities there are special programs offering services for mothers in recovery. The support and practical help they provide can make a difference in day-to-day life for you and your children. Ask your local CAS if such a program is available in your area.

If you continue to use drugs, your CAS caseworker will question your ability to care for your child. Taking good care of a child demands alertness, attention, patience and good judgment. Drugs can affect all these qualities. Using drugs doesn't necessarily make you a bad parent, but it does make it harder to be a good parent.

" Methadone saved my life, and it saved my baby too. When I found out I was pregnant, I tried to go cold turkey, but I couldn't take it and it turned out it was killing the baby. I came to the clinic here, and right away they put me on methadone.

I was clean when the baby was born, and I stayed that way, but the children's aid came into the hospital and they said, we're going to apprehend the baby for three months. I was living in a shelter and I had it set up to stay in a shelter that was for moms and babies but they wouldn't let me take him. They had my other two kids too, they got them when I was in jail. I wanted to get them back.

It was hard, I had to prove myself, but after a few months I got my own apartment and I got the baby, and eventually I got my other two kids back. The baby's five now, and he's one smart cookie. Methadone saved us. "

— Valerie, 35
On methadone six years

Menopause

Women approaching menopause on methadone face the same concerns and decisions to make as women not on methadone. The only exception to this rule may be if you experience profuse sweating, which can be a side-effect of methadone. The sweating, in *combination with the hot flashes common to women* going through menopause, can make you feel pretty droopy. Your doctor may be able to suggest steps you can take to deal with some of the discomfort (for example, hormone replacement therapy or other treatments).

8 looking ahead on methadone

8 looking ahead on methadone

How long will I be on methadone?

This is one of the most frequently asked questions, and *one of the most difficult questions to answer.*

There are two different schools of thought concerning length of treatment for methadone clients. One approach looks at methadone treatment as long *term, and possibly indefinite — like insulin treatment* for the person with diabetes. Opioid dependence is explained as a biological disorder, and methadone is the medicine used to treat the condition.

The other approach looks at methadone as a short-term treatment. This approach sees opioid dependence as the result of the person's attempts to solve emotional problems with drugs. When the person who uses opioids learns to deal with problems in other ways, and his or her life becomes stable and happier, there is less reason to look to drugs for help. Methadone treatment is seen as allowing the person the chance to get well

and get his or her life in
order. Once this is accomplished, the person can
then taper off methadone and progress toward a
drug-free life. Short-term methadone treatment is
usually one to two years.

There is truth in the ideas behind both long- and short-
term treatment approaches. Opioid dependence does
change the way the brain works in that it suppresses
the brain's ability to produce our bodies' natural
opioids, endorphins. People who withdraw from
opioids, including methadone, may feel emotionally
low and have trouble sleeping for months after
withdrawal. It's also true that having a supportive
home life, steady employment and a strong desire
to be drug free can help make the period after
withdrawal easier to get through, and less likely
to result in a return to drug use.

You should know that those who withdraw from
methadone after short-term treatment are more
likely to return to drug use than those who stay in
treatment. This is why many doctors and counsellors
encourage clients to stay in methadone treatment
for the long term.

Keep in mind that the dangers associated with
injection drug use include a high risk of HIV and
hepatitis C infection, increased likelihood of criminal
activity and imprisonment, and the danger of death

from overdose. The consequences of long-term methadone treatment, by comparison, are minimal. Long-term use of methadone has no effect on the internal organs, or on thinking. If methadone helps you to lead a normal, active and happy life, then it is well worth the inconvenience, the side-effects, and any possible stigma you may encounter from people who do not understand the nature of your treatment.

I first started the methadone program when I was in my late 20s, now I'm 53. I never thought I'd live this long, much less be on methadone all this time. I've been on so long now, I don't even remember what my life was like before methadone.

Once you're dependent on meth, you become an enthusiastic devotee; it's your best friend. I think that if you get the chance, you should try to quit while you're young and strong. The longer you're on methadone, the harder it is to quit. It's a highly addictive drug.

— Sandy, 53
On methadone 24 years

Everyone has their own experiences. I just want, once I am stabilized, to be tapered down. I cannot see this taking much time. I want to start living my life.

— Jill, 40
On methadone four weeks

Tapering readiness

If you think you might be ready to leave treatment, there are a number of questions you should ask yourself to help you make the decision whether or not you should begin the tapering process. Consider the following questions:

1. Have you been abstaining from illegal drugs, such as heroin, cocaine and speed? Yes ☐ No ☐

2. Do you think you are able to cope *with difficult situations without* using drugs? Yes ☐ No ☐

3. Are you employed or in school? Yes ☐ No ☐

4. Are you staying away from contact with users and illegal activities? Yes ☐ No ☐

5. Have you gotten rid of your *"works"/"outfit"*? Yes ☐ No ☐

6. Are you living in a neighborhood that doesn't have a lot of drug use, and are you comfortable there? Yes ☐ No ☐

7. Are you living in a stable family relationship? Yes ☐ No ☐

8. Do you have non-user friends that you spend time with? Yes ☐ No ☐

9. Do you have friends or family who would be helpful during a taper? Yes ☐ No ☐

10. Have you been participating in counselling that has been helpful? Yes ☐ No ☐

11. Does your counsellor think you are ready to taper? Yes ☐ No ☐

12. Do you think you would ask for help when you were feeling bad during a taper? Yes ☐ No ☐

13. Have you stabilized on a relatively low dose of methadone? Yes ☐ No ☐

14. Have you been on methadone for a long time? Yes ☐ No ☐

15. Are you in good mental and physical health? Yes ☐ No ☐

16. Do you want to get off methadone? Yes ☐ No ☐

The more questions you can honestly answer by checking "yes," the greater the likelihood that you are ready to taper from methadone. Consider that each "no" response represents an area that you probably need to work on to increase the odds of a successful taper and recovery.*

---

*Tapering Readiness Inventory *from Treatment of Opiate Addiction With Methadone: A Counselor Manual,* U.S. Department of Health and Human Services (DHHS) SMA94-2061

(From S. Brummett, R. Dumontet, L. Wermuth, M. Gold, J.L. Sorensen, S. Batki, R. Dennis & R. Heaphy (1986), *Methadone Maintenance to Abstinence: The Tapering Network Project Manual,* University of California, San Francisco.)

> *My next step is to come off. Meth can be very hard to get off of, even if you're on it for a short time. The truth is, the longer you're on it, the harder it is to come off. I know I can do it, but I'm scared.*
>
> — Margaret, 41
> On methadone 10 years

Methadone tapering

The decision to taper off methadone is best made with the support of your doctor and counsellor, friends and family. If you've been on methadone for a long time, you may have stopped seeing your counsellor. Now is a good time to seek out the services of a counsellor once again. Feelings of fear and anxiety are common to clients as they get close to the end of treatment. The risk of relapse is increased. It's important that you prepare for the challenge by setting up a safety net of support.

Learning about what to expect throughout the tapering process can also be helpful in reducing anxiety. The more you know, the less there is to be afraid of.

Methadone tapering works best when done as a slow and gradual reduction in dose, dropping 5 mg every three to 14 days. At this rate there should be very few, if any, physical symptoms during the taper.

Once the dose is lowered to around 20 mg, the tapering may be slowed down to an even more gradual reduction, to reduce or eliminate any symptoms.

Nowadays, most methadone providers will allow you to choose the rate at which your dose is reduced. This gives you more control of the process, and lets you keep withdrawal symptoms to a minimum. The entire process should be given plenty of time. Expect at least six months to a year.

Regardless of whether you have been in methadone treatment for a short or long time, on a high or low dose, the process is the same, and the degree *of difficulty in withdrawing is the same. All clients withdrawing from methadone find the most difficult* stage is at the end of the taper. This is when you are most likely to have to tolerate some symptoms of withdrawal.

Withdrawal from methadone comes on more slowly and may last longer than withdrawal from opioids such as heroin or OxyContin. With tapering, the withdrawal symptoms should be minimal, but you can expect some aching, insomnia and lack of appetite. These symptoms should go away within 10 to 14 days, but beyond that, you may still feel a sense of loss, sadness and sleeplessness that may go on for several months.

Relapse, or return to drug use, is all too common at this time. It's important to recognize the things that might trigger you to use again before it happens. Stay away from old haunts and old friends from your using days. Call on your non-using friends, family or counsellor if you're feeling low, or frustrated or stressed. Keep in mind that after you've been off opioids for a while, your tolerance to their effects is lowered, meaning that what used to be a normal dose is now an overdose. Watch you don't become a sad statistic. Be careful.

Changing your mind

Keep in mind that you don't have to go off methadone. You can change your mind and return to treatment at any point in the tapering process. Maybe you're not ready yet, maybe you'll be ready at a later time, maybe you'll never be ready. Staying on methadone can be the right choice for some. It's up to you. A return to treatment is *not* a failure. If the choice is between being on methadone, or risking a return to a dangerous drug habit, stick to the methadone — it's better for you. It's better for everybody.

After treatment ends

If you decide to go through with the taper, and you
stop taking methadone, it may still take a while for
your body to adjust from long-term opioid use.
Some people have trouble sleeping, and may feel low.
This can go on for as long as months after the end
of the taper. During this period it is important to
maintain and extend your support. Some find that
becoming involved in support groups such as Narcotics
Anonymous can help provide the extra strength to
stay firm in your decision to be drug free. Individual
counselling can also help.

Recovery from drug abuse is not an instant fix. It
takes time; it's a process. What works for you may or
may not work for someone else. The important thing
is to find your own way, and get headed in the
right direction.

important contact numbers

ConnexOntario

1-800-565-8603

ConnexOntario's drug and alcohol registry of treatment
provides information about treatment for drug and alcohol
problems. Call their 24-hour toll-free number to find
the number of the assessment referral centre in your
community.

Methadone Registry

COLLEGE OF PHYSICIANS AND SURGEONS OF ONTARIO

416-967-2600 EXT. **661**
methadoneinfo@cpso.on.ca

The Methadone Registry keeps a list of all doctors authorized
to prescribe methadone in Ontario. Call to find a doctor
offering treatment in your area.

websites *

Access to the Internet is now available through many public libraries. Even if you don't have a computer at home or work, you can still get information from the web. Here is a list of methadone-related sites:

Addiction Treatment Forum

www.atforum.com

With a focus on methadone, this site reports on new developments in the understanding of substance use and treatment. The site is designed both for medical professionals and for clients.

---

* The websites listed here were current when we published this handbook. *If you cannot find the site you are looking for, it may be because it no* longer exists. Try a web search using "methadone resources" if you want *to find one of the many other methadone-related sites that are available.*

Drug Policy Alliance

www.drugpolicy.org

This U.S. drug and drug policy research institute offers
news stories, an online library, discussion forums, listservs
and links to other resources. Type "methadone" into their
search engine.

Drug Text: The Internet's Center
for Substance Use Related Risk Reduction

www.drugtext.org

This Dutch drug policy and human rights organization
provides "globally accessible drug-related information."
A search of the site's "libraries" will lead you to dozens of
online references on methadone, including a methadone
client handbook from the U.K.

The International Center for Advancement
of Addiction Treatment

www.opiateaddictionrx.info

This site provides thoroughly researched information, news
and views about methadone and other addiction issues.

Methadone Anonymous

www.methadone-anonymous.org

The Methadone Anonymous (MA) site supports the work of MA groups wherever they are founded. The site provides *specific information for those who want to start their own* MA group. MA is a 12-step recovery group that accepts methadone as a "therapeutic tool of recovery that may or may not be discontinued in time, depending upon the needs of the individual."

The Methadone Site

www.geocities.com/themethadonesite/

The stated aim of this U.S. site is to "educate the world's population about methadone maintenance and *detoxification." The site includes lots of links and active* message boards.

Methadone Today

www.methadonetoday.org

The official newsletter of the Detroit Organizational Needs in Treatment, a methadone advocacy group. The newsletter offers links to other websites, articles by methadone clients on a range of methadone issues, plus a doctor's column answering questions about treatment. The website also offers information on starting a Methadone Anonymous group.

The National Alliance
of Methadone Advocates

www.methadone.org

A U.S. organization of clients and supporters of MMT. Their primary objective is to get rid of stigma and empower the methadone client.

notes